Love Poems TO GOD

FROM DARKNESS TO LIGHT

SHERYL WALKER

authorHOUSE®

AuthorHouse™
1663 Liberty Drive
Bloomington, IN 47403
www.authorhouse.com
Phone: 1 (800) 839-8640

Published by AuthorHouse 08/09/2019

ISBN: 978-1-7283-2235-3 (sc)
ISBN: 978-1-7283-2234-6 (e)

Library of Congress Control Number: 2019911235

Print information available on the last page.

Broken open
For creativity to flow out
Is the gift of pain
Thank you pain

See God in every moment
Move through the darkness
Reflect
Emerge stronger than ever
Awake in the dawn

Drown out the voices of discouragement
And despair
It's all a blessing
All of it

Have complete dependence on Him
He says lay down your burdens onto me
Really do that
Because you can't handle them alone

Forgive yourself and those that came before you
For inadequate healing
Now begin healing

Dedication

She prayed
She prayed
She prayed

Bernice prayed
Felicia prayed
Joyce prayed
Lynwood prayed
Mattie prayed

We are living in the bounty of our
Grandmothers' prayers
They prayed for the lineage
They prayed for the generations

They prayed
They prayed
They prayed

Acknowledgements

Thank you to my family,
friends, and fellow writers
that provided feedback
Forever grateful

Contents

THE DAWN   85

THE LIGHT 127

Sitting by the window sill

God,
Seldom words describe your love
No description to adequately capture your magnitude
Maybe the sun comes close
Sitting by the window sill in admiration
At the consistency of dawn
And the consistency of dusk

As the peppermint tea bag seeps
In the white china with the blue floral trim
With the matching saucer
I have too much water in my tea cup
And it runs over

My gaze locks
And I am left speechless
By the majestic monarch butterfly
Gold and black
Black and gold
Landing so delicately on the red rose bud
Both intricately detailed
Each stage of the metamorphosis
With a prescribed purpose
Who else but the miraculous savior
The omnipotent master creator

Then the pain of my carpal tunnel aches
The left wrist throbs
There is pulsation with abnormal rapidity
And I remember He too is a healer
The pain lingers but it's faint
While His track record is not

Meanwhile, the red cardinal begins foraging for food
And just like that, the cardinal finds it
You will always find it
"It," whatever it be, is always supplied

Prince of peace
Lord of Lords
Comforter through times of fear
Protector while under siege
Burden bearer when the trials became too heavy
Energizer when the spirit is low
Hope giver when all hope is gone
Vindicator when they don't mean us well
Battle fighter when Goliath gets too big
Source of strength in times of weariness
The help in times of trouble
The forgiver of all sin and
The orchestrator of all good things
The commitment to your promises
The love you have for us
Grace and mercy giver
Blessings supplier

Like air
The everything, the everywhere
The meeter of all needs

Moments of splendor
And moments of simplicity
Like sitting by the window sill
Drinking peppermint tea
In the white china with the blue floral trim
With the matching saucer

Unconditional
L-O-V-E
Even while undeserving
Steady, firm, and rooted
Like the red rose bud
The majestic monarch butterfly lands upon
Gold and black
Black and gold
Right outside the window sill
Right
Outside
The window sill

My Lord
My God
My everything
The one sure thing

God, seldom words describe your love...

The Dark

Abandoned
Alone
Angry
Anxious
Apathetic
Arrogant
Attached
Battles
Beat down
Betrayed
Break up
Broken-hearted
Broken open
Challenges
Change
Complaining
Confused
Death
Demotion
Dependence
Destroyed
Disappointed
Discouraged
Dishonest
Distractions
Divorce
Doubt
Ego
Envy
Evil
Expectations

False associations
False pride
Fear
Fighting for acceptance
Fighting for inclusion
Fighting to be heard
Frozen in pain
God
God's presence
Goliath
Greed
Grudges
Guilt
Idols
Imprisonment
Inferiority
Infertility
Intimidation
Jealousy
Judgement
Lies
Loss
Overwhelmed
Pain
Persecuted
Phoniness
Politics
Pride
Regret
Rejection
Resentment

Run down
Self-Pity
Separation
Shame
Sickness
Sideswiped
Sin
Sorrow
Spiritual Attack
Stagnation
Stress
Struck down
Superiority
Survival
Tests
The enemy
The insecure
The past
The weapons
Trauma
Tribulations
Victimhood
Void
Wasting away
Weakness
Weapons
Who has courage anymore?
Worry
Yearning

1

Blackout

Murky, muted, and frozen
Disoriented and unsure
Digging myself out of deep, dark crevices

Pain please teach me all the lessons
Before you go
So that when you revisit
I will know what to do, at least partially
Dreaming of a victory

The blackout is where we grow the most
Thank you for the opposition
The tribulation

Rejoice in the now
Victory is near
Electricity shall be restored

#2

Act

Float along, lazy river
Muddy torment my caregiver

Green willowed trees frame my respite
Silence summoning summer crickets, desperate
For high tides to envelop my common sense
Wishing fingers crossed, eyes closed shut, at others expense

Abandon the fallacy of faith without action
Dive in and swim
Pick up barreling traction

Swim against the current, fighter fish
The feast of intimidation, a favorite dish

Brave soldiers keep windows of courage ajar
Bleak, barren prospects, but still a North Star

#3

The tunnel

Hope, where are you?
In the tunnel of faith
All I have is belief
Confined
Claustrophobia kicking in
Are you sure the end is in sight?

Then I hear a whisper,
"Sometimes the only way out is through
Maximize the moment you are currently in"

Awareness of God is the
Optimism and hope in unrealistic conditions
This is the hardest battle

#4

A woodpecker's feast

I'm tired of that stinging feeling
You are trying to hurt me again
Every slight
Every jab
Stabbed quickly
The holes don't penetrate deep enough
For me to bleed out
But the body is like a piece of wood
A woodpecker has feasted on for days
On end
Drilling into me
But not enough to break me in half
But still not completely whole
Punctured, bruised, trauma to the soul
I'm so tired of that stinging feeling

#5

Perpetual strength

All is for good
Even when they reject me

All is for good
Even when they slander my name

Even in the midst of the attacks,
You give me rest

A marathon
Of perpetual strength

Pressing on
Despite the opposition

#6

Ahead

Looking over the balcony
the aerial view allows me to see
The path made clear
All that is
And all that will be
The man on the copper bicycle
Will encounter a stop sign
Two blocks north

When the enemy sees what is ahead
He will try whatever he can to discourage
The enemy will use any one in our lives
Kin, next of kin, strangers
No one gets away

No retaliation needed
You will always end up in the winning position
Despite it all
I have you Lord
And you will never hurt me with words or actions
In fact,
You constantly remind me of the many reasons

Why you love me
Vast and vigorous is your love

They will aim their thorny turbulent darts
Unpleasant and unyielding
But they will not win

SHERYL WALKER

#7

Pain then blessing

I thought I was a has been
Washed up
Bent out of shape
Broken
But built
What good will come out of this, I ask?
How can pain be beneficial?

Aggravated and agitated
Approach tribulations with a deep knowing
Something good will come out of this

God, what is the treasure in this trial?
Fallen
Forgotten
Fearful
I know this won't last forever
All is temporary

Is anything too hard for God?
All is possible through Him

I've lived this pattern before
Pain
Blessing
Pain
Blessing

SHERYL WALKER

#8

Sturdy

Built like brass
Ferocious as a tornado
Sturdy as a statue

Break the strongholds
In my life, God
Let me become intolerant to the sin in my life

Let the valley not be self-inflicted
By wants and desires
Wash it away in the rainstorm, God

9

Forest fires

Concrete peace wall
Impenetrable
Happy bubble

Stop giving over your life to others
Do not allow them to
Occupy your mental space

Engulf your joy
Like a campfire in the forest
Unconquerable flame
Mind destroyed
You must
Persist

SHERYL WALKER

#10

Repeat offender

I'm searching for the courage
To lay aside the hatred and hurt
And to respect the
Good in that person
Especially an enemy
Who continues to hurt me

At least give me a chance to let the wound heal
How do I forgive
A repeat offender?
I want to heal
I want to forgive
We are all human
Hurt by others, meanwhile
Hurting others
The twisted human experience

#11

Forgive

The lapse of time
Frees you from
The commitment
To the offense

Lord please give me the strength to forgive
You constantly forgive me

The impact of the offense is still so fresh
Just like a mosquito bite
Or the sting of a bee
How do you restore the trust?
How do I press on?
Keep a smile on my face?
A facade of perfection
Hopeful and optimistic
In the face of opposition
Is that not leadership?

I don't want to get so busy
Hiding the pain
Keeping the mask on tight
That no one sees the truth
Even me

#12

The test

Tribulations are life's trust test

(1) Can I let go and let God fight my battles?
(2) Can I remain present and positive?
(3) Can I identify the blessing in the midst of the pain?
   (The sun is shining. I am alive.)
(4) Will I continue to dwell on situations and circumstances?
(5) Will I wait pleasantly?

#13

The enemy

Naive and needy
Never giving God
The credit He deserves
I cleave to the noise
And distraction of man
Obedient to the outrageous
Enemy
Liar
Thief
The offended
The abused
Anxious
Supporter of sin
Promoter of division
Frozen in pain
The victim
The flesh
Lingering distress
The residue of the offense
Doubt
I rebuke thee
Ego
Selfish ego
Make me big

Make them love me
I am in control
It was me
the talents
the gifts
the strength
It was me
Me, me, me
It was all me
Untouchable
Overlooked
Overdue

#14

This world

I pray for our world
Where the tide of atheism is rising
Where we hold onto
Temporary things

Making sense of this world means
God first
Life is now
There are no do overs
Nothing is by chance
Nothing

There are times when patience will be required
The waiting period is agonizing
There are many mistakes
You will make them
Others will make them
And you will be impacted
And you must forgive

Nothing will fill you like God
Nothing
Never stop learning
Engaging in good conversation
The opportunities
They come
The miracles
They arrive in unexpected form

#15

Trust in God

All of the time
Not just the good times
But even in the bad times
With all of my heart
Not my limited understanding
Obey His instructions
Opportunity wrapped in obedience
Sensitivity to the Holy Spirit
Your gut instinct
That still small voice
What is the last thing He told you to do?
They will send for you
You will be the answer to the problem
You will be there as a servant
You already have God's approval to be there
Appointed in private
Even when you regress
It is just a test
Humble enough to start over again
He goes from glory to glory

Don't miss it
Humble yourself
Purpose is tied to a place
Not the person
The place
The assignment
Live in obedience

#16

Helpless despair

Caught like a mouse's tail in the trap
The enemy wants you to feel helpless
And in despair
What is the message
Through these tears?
Listen and obey
Trust the Lord
With all your heart
Do not lean
On your own understanding
God will guide you

SHERYL WALKER

#17

Stronger Faith

I will stand firm in my faith
He has our back in every situation
In extremely difficult times
When God seems to be unfaithful
When your faith is breaking
That is when God is actually
Making your faith stronger

#18

Never doubt

You will be stronger
If you win over the temptation
To doubt him
Everything happens
For a reason
In due season
Think back at a holy miracle
I know you didn't
Expect that to happen
When it did
The way that it did
Now did you?

#19

God's plans

Cement saturated
It is set in stone

Take notice:
What is for you
Is for you
No one can take that away
No one can change God's divine plan
Not a single soul
Trust, faith, hope, belief

#20

Let go

The tattered teddy bear
I held onto for dear life…
It is painful to release comfort
But God might be saying to us, trust me…
Allow yourself to go through this painful season,
Because what I have
On the other side of this hardship
Is something even better
It will knock your socks off
Just trust me
The testing of your faith
Is a part of my plan for you
Keep shedding your dependency on all things
Other than me
Fear of acceptance
Fear of approval
Like the locust
Release the wants and desires

All you have right now
Is really all you need right now

SHERYL WALKER

#21

It's manifesting

Agonized
Aching
Beat down
In the boxing ring of life

Afraid
Hurt like a fly over swatted but never killed
I crave peace within my soul
The peace in the silent knowing that
All is well
All is for my good
God's perfect will is manifesting
I will let God fight my battles
So grand and colossal
You take care of it all
Lord you take care of it all

#22

Covered

Apprehensive
Angry
Anxious and
Alienated
But anchored
Lord let me not be intimidated by the threats of bullies
I am covered
By the full armor of God

Envy
Jealousy
Power
Attention
Is often the reason behind the bully
There is nothing
Absolutely nothing
They can do to my core being
I will save my fear for God
He knows the number of hairs on my head
Don't you think He will care for me too?

#23

Light

Ambitious
Artistic
Antique
Shine your light
But the haters
Joy snatchers
Insecure
Candle snuffers
Want to suppress
Out your flame
Don't let them

#24

He is for me

Bland
Bogus
Bare
Bleak
Barren
Evil deeds come from evil people
Fear quickly becomes hate
Even when your enemies plan your destruction
God will have someone there to help you
God is for you
So no enemy will win
God has the final say
Rest assured
You were positioned to be there

#25

Unstable

Exhausted and frayed
I surrender
Every detail
Every constant change
Once I feel firm
A plank goes loose
The rug gets pulled from under my feet
I surrender all of it
I am nothing without you
I am totally dependent on you
Everlasting Lord

#26

Always present

Generous Lord
I exalt your name
Only your glory can fill this place
Envelop every empty space in my life
With your presence
I yearn for you Lord
Make yourself known
I am gripping and grabbing for any piece of you
Your warmth
Your comfort
The knowing that
You are always with me
Despite my human
External conditions
You are always with me
Graceful and grandiose God
You are always with me

#27

Get through

Grim outlook
Feelings of shame
Life can knock us off our feet
Figuratively and
Literally
Every fiber of our physical and emotional being
Heavy, anchor heavy
Someone has to help me out
Of this valley
Anxious
Praying for relief
The hope is to
Just
Get
Through
Blessings are on the other side
You
Will
Get
Through
Hope is on the way

#28

Focus

With the kaleidoscope of burdens
Focusing is unlikely
Overwhelmed by circumstance
That is both awful and alarming
Focus on God
He is greater than any mountain
Any challenge
Nothing stands a chance against
Our mighty God

SHERYL WALKER

#29

Where are you God?

Defeated and filled with despair
Stay in the game of life
Lord equip me where I am weak
Fill the holes in my knowledge,
Ability, and experience
He knows your weaknesses
Fully aware of your lack
Your struggle in the dark
Let me be reminded
Of how much you love me
During the times I feel unloved
Be my one-on-one tutor
Show me where I need to grow
And provide the right teacher
In the midst of my dismay,
Lord please keep me encouraged
Past experiences tell me
That when I am discouraged,
Extremely tempted
Breakthrough is on the way
Keep me pressing forward
Lavish me with your love
Not losing personal confidence
When the battle gets tough

Should I be more aggressive?
Should I take more of a stand?
Should I exert more confidence?
If that is so,
Lord build me up
Push me beyond my own limitations

SHERYL WALKER

#30

Sickness

Sickness oh sickness
How did you get here?
You linger like roaches
Annoying
Invasive
And always around
When the light turns on
You make your presence abound

#31

When?

The abused abuse others
When will the cycle end?

My lack
Becomes the impetus
For me to inflict pain on others
When will the cycle end?

SHERYL WALKER

#32

The Source

I fight not forgetting
The source of my strength
Armor up in prayer
Remember God's past faithfulness
His greatness
The biblical miracles
Let your words be measured
Stop and think
How He brought the
Ordinary and overlooked seedling
Into a beautiful enchanting azalea
Radiant
Regal and
Remarkable

Always Faithful

Vivid violet nightingale
"Has God ever left you before?"
He will never ever leave you
Pray and the way shall be revealed
Keep on believing
And the path will be made clear
God is always faithful

Faith asks again
"Has God ever left you before?"
He will never leave you
Pray and the way shall be revealed
Keep on believing
God loves you
He is always faithful

SHERYL WALKER

#34

Unbearable pain

Wisdom tooth pulled
The throbbing
As the novocain wears off
Pain, agonizing pain
At times so unbearable

Trust God
Even through the discomfort of worry
Even in the dark places
Even in the anxious places
Even in the overwhelmed
And troubling places
Trust God

#35

Eye of the storm

The winds
The waves
The storms
Your pain and agony
Is connected to the next blessing

Right before the miracle,
You will experience devastation
Frustration
Aggravation
Irritation

Something amazing must be near
Anchored to hope
In the eye of the storm
And then the breakthrough
In that order
Storm
Then breakthrough
What will you sacrifice?

#36

The past trap

What goes unspoken
Is the story behind the story

Save me from my sins Lord
The sins that keep me bound in guilt
The sins that linger in my mind
That pop up at the most
Unwanted times

The past is a trap
That will leave you in bondage
Stuck like glue

You can't change the past
You can try to heal the wounds

#37

The unknown

As the hail of silence
And the thunder of not knowing
Dwindle down to the
Wind chimes of certainty
Who controls it all?

The answer seems vague

Be comfortable not knowing what's next
Your humanity may cause you to question God
But you cannot remain upset
He is the only one that can help you
Only God
And God alone

#38

Bad news

Vicious villain
Carrier of despair
Bad news, Bad news
You don't frighten me
It stings
Blindsided
But in time, I will make it

Up the mountain with all my might
I can overcome any problem
Through Christ
I shall not be afraid of bad news
No problem shall separate me
From Christ's unfailing
And everlasting love
He will comfort me
Envelop me in his arms

Faith

Childlike faith
Waiting in wonder
And expectation
Mover of mountains
Upright, strong, and unmoved
Complete and absolute trust
Undistracted by the winds of circumstance
The how is God's job
Requests, already on their way
Knowing that all is for good
And for a reason
Faith doesn't look like perfection
Or a feeling of comfort
Or what feels like a necessity
Faith tells us not to quit
But to stay the course
Until God says move
Faith produces patience
The will to persevere

Peace, joy, an inner confidence
A greater purpose
All for His glory
Eternity
Then he will say,
Job well done
My humble servant

#40

Difficulties

Like footprints imprinted in the sand
Trust the God who knows every step of our way
Even through difficulties
We must learn to trust him
The lesson of trust
Is wrapped in difficulties
Spiritual blessings
Come masked as trials
So trust him
He has the ability to
Bend time
And events
In your favor
He is the
Invisible hand
Holding you
Even with possibility
In blindfolds

#41

Worry

How futile it is to worry
Even in the uncertainty
There is certainty
Fear and worry
Rob us of an abundant life
Everything you worry about will work out

#42

Working

When you bring your requests to God
Trust He will always do
What is best
God is with us
God works in everything
God is working now
Not on our happiness
But to fulfill His purpose
No matter what
We can never be separated
From God's unfailing love

#43

Always Faithful

Even in the valley of discouragement
My faith tells me
The only constant in life is God
He will always show up and
Do what He says He will do
There is no doubt in my heart
That He is with me
And will do what is best for me
Always faithful
Always consistent
He plants the dream
And brings it to fruition in ways
I could never imagine
During His right time

New battle?
Don't forget His past faithfulness
Worry and faith are opposites
You can't worry and have faith
You have to choose one
I choose faith

#44

Strength

A never-ending reservoir of Samson strength
God will never tell you to do something
That won't work out for your good
Just get through it
And try to remain pleasant
Along the way

#45

Suffering

How will I handle this suffering?
In the valley
Alone
Feeling lost
In the depths of rejection
Where are you God?
The anger
Grief
Fear
Despair
Take me under

I complain to you God
And only you
Because only you can rescue me

And then that still small voice
Reminds me that you are
Always working
You never leave us
You will never forsake us

#46

For the kingdom

Don't make God feel regret
I want God to say job well done
In response to
My grace
Mercy
And
Forgiveness
Eternal life will be oh so sweet
God will say
"You have made me so proud"
When harboring unforgiveness
Stop and remember
This is kingdom work
It was never about you
Let it go

#47

Still standing

The only reason I am standing is because of
The grace of God
Nothing is by my
Own doing

It is His direction
Protection, and
Divine plan for my life

Who am I to bemoan the pain?
If He overcame the world, then
So can I

Accept the rejection
Until acceptance

He is the soothing aloe
To the burn of the beating sun

He has me in the palm of His hands
Covered in safety

#48

Offense

Worn down
Broken
Bumpy
Like days old fruit
Left out on the kitchen counter

Learn not to be offended
By every slight and
Cold shoulder
Being offended won't change anything
And won't do you any good
The problem is the flesh

#49

Motive

Attention Soldier,
The work God has assigned for you
Is difficult work
You will be like sheep running
Through a wolf pack
As cunning as a snake
Inoffensive as a dove
Constantly asking
What is their motive?

#50

The plea

Run down
Beat down
Beyond belief
Ask and it shall be given
It is said, you have not
Because you ask not
God here is my request
Here is my plea
Here is the problem
In its simplicity
The enemy is attacking me
Devil, flee!
Jesus help me
I am your servant
I bring my problems to you
If I keep them inside
The burden becomes more
Than I can bear

#51

All things

I can do all things
I
Can do all things
I can
Do all things
I can do all
Things
I can do all things
Through Christ
Who strengthens me

#52

Lead me

A compass
Direct me God
Guide me
Be my map
My eternal GPS

God has you
He got you out
And pointed you in the right direction
Exactly where you needed to go

He is able to do
Above and beyond
Anything we could ever hope for

#53

His hands

Solid and attached
He's got the whole world
In His hands
The outcome
Is completely in God's control
Proceed with humility
Remember your past victories
Listen
For His voice
Approach with reverence

#54

Purpose

On the battlefield
Swords drawn
Stay close to God
In constant communication
If your purpose is to go to war
Don't lose sight of your purpose

When it is time to exit
God will show you to the door
But until then
Show up to the battle ground
Armored in His presence
His biblical miracles
His past faithfulness
His greatness
Let your words be measured
Stop
Think
Strategize

SHERYL WALKER

#55

Temptation

Demolish the strongholds, God
When temptation comes,
The lust
The flesh
The eyes
The wants and desires
Help me to turn away
To flee from it
Or it will consume me
And there are dire consequences
Very dire consequences attached

#56

Sin

Don't be an accomplice to sin
What is my part?
Where is my repentance?
What is God's will?

SHERYL WALKER

#57

Unbearable

Drowning in dismay
Pain can be so unbearable
But God will comfort us
He is the chief burden bearer
The sun will shine again
One day precious God
One day

#58

Focus

Wind
Grass
Dandelions
Velvet sailboat
Chaotic lily pad
Anything that makes you anxious
Is a growth opportunity
Come back to the present
Focus on God

#59

Present

Gratitude protects us from negative thinking
Stay present and in the now
Each day has its own burdens
God is always next to you
Holding your hand

#60

These bags

There is a burden of guilt
I am carrying and I cannot bear it anymore
The burden of unintentionally hurting
Those I love
It is a heavy burden to carry
I need grace and mercy delivered
To free myself of this load
Please let me know I am forgiven
Just a smile
Just a call
Just an invitation
Back into your life

SHERYL WALKER

#61

Get through

Lent
Left
Hidden
Abandoned
Washed up
On the side of the ally
There are consequences for our actions
But you still come around and save us
From our sins

Lost
Torn
Worn
Trusting that whatever God sends my way,
He will give me what I need to get through it

#62

Armored up

Enter the lion's den
Fully armored in prayer
Hungry
Angry
Lonely
Tired
Sick
Protect yourself
From the leeches
You must
Charge up
Plan your escape route

#63

Heavy bags

Victim or abuser?
Both carry very heavy bags
And very heavy burdens

#64

Memories

The trap of our memories
It happened the way it did
Exactly the way it was supposed to
Press forward

#65

Timing

Notice the enemies timing
Set to defeat us
Set to prevent the glorious
Works of God to manifest
We have to put our trust in God
Not man
Be mindful of timing

#66

Warfare

Swords, grenades, and bayonets
As you get closer to God
Closer to a healing
The spiritual warfare will increase

#67

Still

Lay down your cares on God
Seek His face
Be still
Relax
Let go
Keep striving
Follow the prompting

#68

Healing

How do I
Perceive
Process
Respond to this
Trauma
That lingers?
Where is my healing?
In the darkest moment
Where is the light?

SHERYL WALKER

#69

Hiding

Behind a bush
God, I hide in shame
For my thoughts, words, and deeds
Have not been right
I know they have consequences
When it isn't right and according to your will,
Like Adam and Eve
I want to hide
But I know you are all knowing
Thank you for
Seeing me as who I ought to be
Through the eyes of my best

#70

Fear

Lord I will lean on you
To be my strength
Fear oh fear
I rebuke thee
I trust you Jesus
At all times
Despite appearances
You have all the power and glory
And limitless love for me

#71

Down for a bit

The enemy is predictable
He will overwhelm you with family sickness,
Despair
When your family elevates,
Then you become sick
Remember all is for good
God reigns supreme
Even when you are down for a bit
God is giving you time to
Prepare in the waiting

The Dawn

Abundance
Boundaries
Deliverance
Forgiveness
God
God I'm ready
God's presence
Growth
Healing
His promises
His strength
Hope
Moving past the pain
Obedience
Opportunities
Perspective
Pressing on
Provision
Ready for God to use my life
Reconciliation
Renewed hope
Replenished
Restored
Strength
Submission
Surrender
The armor of God
The end of addiction
The end of dependency
The plea
The waiting
Through the dark
Unseen forces
Victory

#1

The beach

There is a rocking motion to the beach
We don't see the shoreline
Recede over time
Because we are lulled not to take notice of
The small changes

The tides are turning in the waiting
We may not see it
But God is always in motion
Even in the stillness
The rocking
The lull

SHERYL WALKER

#2

You can't change people

Take people off your "to do" list
Wishing someone
Was who we desire
Them to be

Take people off your "to change" list
More like this
Less like that
Free them of your limiting
Expectations

God changes people
Not us
Vengeance is His
Not ours

We are told to love people
Not change people
We are told to pray for people
And leave them in God's hands

They are
Divinely
And perfectly
Made
Leave all of the refinements to God

#3

Closed for healing

Wash wound
Apply the ointment
Band-Aid on
Lord I thank you for periods of
Rest
Healing
Restoration
A time to turn inward and reflect
Limited abuse coming in
Please God give me a period of
REST
From my enemies
Band-Aid on
Silence
Breath
Phoenix rising
Fiercer now
Because I endured

#4

Beat up ragdoll

On the continuum of
About to enter pain
In pain
Or
Just left pain and closed
For healing
But we rarely close for healing long enough
So we take our
Pained
Run down selves
Into new painful experiences

SHERYL WALKER

#5

Gratitude

We don't notice the good days
Like we remember the bad days
We complain about the cold days of winter
And the sweltering days of summer
Bemoan the rain
But rarely show gratitude
For the dawn of each new day
Its consistency
The fact that we are alive

#6

Ego

Chest puffed
Ego, where are you?
Because when I'm filled with pride
I blow everything out of proportion
Wherever there is conflict, there is pride
Who didn't win this time?
Who is going to be brave enough to let it go this time?
Ego blocks us from seeing life clearly
What God is doing in our lives

#7

Recovery

You cannot change people, but
You can recover
With or without them
This too shall pass
God has the final say
What are the lessons in this moment?
One day this will be irrelevant
Pain heals
There is a bigger picture and purpose
To your present place

#8

Ready

I am
Available to do whatever
You want for me to do
With my life

I am
Ready to give my time
Money
And spirit

I am
Ready to live a life
Devoted to serving
You

I am
Ready to humble myself
And sacrifice all
Wholeheartedly
For your glory

I am
Ready to do
All
That is acceptable
In your sight
Lord, I am ready

#9

Is it you?

If it isn't you,
I don't want anything to do with it
If you are not in it,
I don't want to be in it
Take my name off the list
If it is not sent by you
Only from you, God
Only sent by you

#10

Focus on God

The release
The wooh sah in the child's pose
When anxious
Be grateful
God has never left you
Hide in His presence
Always there
Behind the stillness of the clouds
Let His loving arms envelop you
His confident peace
Submerge you in His river of love
Nothing can harm you
Shift away from your problems and plans
Focus on God

#11

Disappointment

During the wait
Disappointment sets in
"When God, when?"
The waiting is the hardest
God says, "You can be disappointed in me,
But never stop trusting me."
God shows up where faith is present
You have to
Believe
God will do
What he says He will do
When
He says He will do it

#12

My seat is waiting

He loves me completely
Has a purpose for my life
Has a seat waiting for me in eternity
For now, I will
Pray
Read His word
Wait patiently
Praise and worship
With complete devotion
Thank Him in advance
Seek wisdom
Keep the belt of truth buckled
Around my waist
The breastplate of righteousness
Intact
The helmet of salvation
Positioned just right
The sword of the spirit
Concealed but ever present
Not take on every battle
Feed my mind with what pleases Him
Remain present
Free myself from the guilt
And shame of the past
Seize opportunities
To be a blessing to others
Ooze with love

#13

Obey

What was the last thing God told you to do?
Do whatever it is He told you to do
What are His commands?
Even if it seems illogical
I don't know why He chose me
He often calls the unqualified
Submit and have faith
Obedience
He will do what you ask him to do
The obedience of faith
You will see a miracle in your life

#14

The perils of pain

To still be soft
Despite a life that could make you hard
Is beautiful
And courageous

To be like a child and
Know the world is safe
That you are loved
You are who you are supposed to be
And where you are supposed to be
God is
And will be
You are free
To be peace filled
To be loving to yourself and all others
Give praise and thanksgiving for everything
E-V-E-R-Y-T-H-I-N-G

#15

Opportunity

Alert
Koi fish
Swimming around the pond
Engaged in playful banter
A tap on the shoulder
Spins you around
Who was that?
What was that?

Opportunity, opportunity
You appear out of the thin blue sky
A continuous series of miraculous
Open windows in the face of closed doors
God's will for our lives
Is expressed through you
But, is this from God or an obstruction?
A blessing or a lesson?
God I'm listening

SHERYL WALKER

#16

Forgivable

I hear everything is forgivable
Everything can heal
All wounds
That you can move past the pain
Time
Space
The right therapist
Lots of tears
Even more prayer
The right positive outlets
But you must do the work
I am hopeful

#17

Healing

Above the trenches of muddy water
The lotus flower blooms
Remarkable beauty
Purity of heart and mind

Pray
Write
Do the work
Forgive
Commit to new behaviors
Consult wise counsel
Hold your tongue
Approach each day with positive expectation
Forget the past
Be open to the possibility of miracles
Even the time sensitive miracles
A better day is ahead
You will be replenished
You will be restored

#18

Life's winners and losers

She always kept up photos of key life events-the marriages,
the babies, the graduations
This numbs the pain through the challenging moments
You win when you can dwell on the good moments
You win when you keep a smile on your face
You win when you persevere despite the setback
You win when you truly enjoy the company of others, loving
the undeserving
You win when you can laugh at life and yourself
You win when you keep singing and dancing despite it all

#19

Broken

Many are walking around
Broken
Hurt
Traumatized
Or just not fully whole
How do I heal
Without simultaneously
Inflicting pain on those that
Love me?

SHERYL WALKER

#20

Up to you

To heal you have to
Put in the work
Take the first step
And the second
Third
Fourth
Your healing is up to you
Not up to the one
Who inflicted it

#21

<u>What heals?</u>

Kindness heals pain
Put yourself in the midst
Of very kind people

Venting can heal
A response can heal
A text can heal
You would be surprised
At all that heals

#22

Words

My words have power
To bless
To curse
Thoughts turn into words
Words turn into deeds
Monitor my own self talk
Now

#23

Heal yourself

I am waiting for an apology
From the abuser
Heal your own self
That is not their responsibility
I dictate the healing
I always had the power
It rests within me
Sometimes lack of closure
Is the closure
Life goes on
With or without you
You can stay stuck
Or embrace each
New day
For the gift
That it is

SHERYL WALKER

#24

How to approach each day

Hope in the day
Be positive
Be kind
Get closer to God
Talk to him
Praise him
Thank him

Work hard
Admire the sun shining
Be optimistic
Step back and learn
Pivot your attention
To that which deserves it

God gives us grace
To face each new day
Every day has its own worries
Every day has its own blessings
Every day has its own miracles

#25

Change

Little acorn
You have the potential
To be a mighty forest
With the tiniest faith
Lord I plead the blood
A blessing is on its way
I will get ready
As you set the scene
The miracle is coming
The tides are turning
All in my favor

SHERYL WALKER

Kind, in spite of cruelty

Life is funny
You are to be kind
Even when others aren't kind to you

Kill them with kindness
They say
Even if they are killing you

But you can only
Overcome evil with good
Remember that

When you are kind
In spite of cruelty
And somehow
Remain whole
You are a unicorn
Or a half decent person

Thank you, God,
For opportunities
To show kindness
Even in the midst
Of evil

The cycles of life

Have you forgotten all
God has done?

Life is cyclical
Hurt
Happiness
Hurt
Happiness
Wait for it
It is going to cycle back around

#28

Living

I see the hustle
And bustle
Of coming and going
In our own worlds
In our own minds
The movie reel of
Yesterday
The what ifs of the past
The trepidation and anxiety
Of the future
Crashing into each other
Snapping
Misinterpreting
Building stories
Constructing lies
Peace be still
Live in the now
They didn't mean to hurt you

#29

Compliments

I was tired once
And I got a good word
The word said
Keep your candle lit
The word said
You are a breath of fresh air
Those words energized me
Gave me fresh new strength

#30

The knowing

Please God
Cover me
Protect me
Envelop me in your arms
I feel anxious
I feel afraid
But I trust you
This feeling will pass
Things will work out for my good
Please God give me peace
Give me the peace that surpasses
All understanding
Ease my mind
Ease my worries

Healing 101

What does healing look like?
First, it's the wall
An unquestionable boundary
I won't let you hurt me anymore
A brick wall covers this
Fresh open wound

Second, it's the beginning
Of my healing
I will write
I will sing
I will dance
These are the bandages
And the ointment

Third, it's the scab
People will test you
Pick at your scab
Don't fall for it
Your healing is on the line

Last, it's the scar
It reminds you
There was trauma here
But even scars can heal

SHERYL WALKER

#32

Worst times

No matter the circumstance,
God is with us
Life is challenging
He will give us the strength to get
Through it
But when we reflect,
Didn't the best learning happen
Through the
Worst times?

#33

Love prayer

Lord I am your beloved child
Angels sang in jubilation when I was born
I am wonderfully made
I have an inheritance
I have favor
The purpose you have for my life has already been ordained

Lord I pray for increased patience
To model mercy and grace
I will love others as I love myself
I will love based on nothing
But them being your child, Father
Not based on favoritism
To either the poor or the great

Lord grant me acceptance
Please allow me to meet people where they are
Fully accepting their limitations
And figuring out ways to work around my own limitations
Let others see the full potential you see in them

SHERYL WALKER

Lord teach me to love my neighbor as myself
To purposefully pray for others
To show genuine care for others
Allow me not to personalize the actions of others
Allow me to love through it all

Lord, help me to consciously choose
Joy and happiness
Help me to rejoice always
Even in difficult situations
Let me not allow circumstances or situations
To steal my joy
I will accept all tribulations
As a message from you to draw nearer
No matter what
Let me choose to rejoice anyhow

Lord empower me to live in my purpose
And not to compare myself to others
Understanding you have equipped us all
With various gifts and talents

Lord, please help me to exercise discipline in my life
Help me to become an expert giver
And an expert forgiver
Remembering no past mistake
Will mar my beauty
I will not let my past
Kill my dreams, peace, joy, or perspective
My past is just that
I will move forward in faith and hope

I will love my enemies
And pray for those that persecute me
And "appear" to bring me harm

I will not judge others
Understanding everyone has their own unique path
I will not personalize others' judgments of me
That is where they are on their journey
God is working on them
As He is working on me

Thank you for those you deliberately place in my life
To love me, encourage me,
And even those sent to teach me painful,
But valuable lessons, Father.

I am going to love and praise you
With all of my heart
And all of my soul
Those who bless me
God you will bless

Let me remain silent
When there isn't a need for a response
For it is an expression of their own pain and
Never a need to retaliate

Allow me to feel safe enough
To be vulnerable
Allow love to reign

I will meditate only on those things that are true and lovely
I disassociate with negativity, Lord

Thank you for your righteousness
I want to stay right beside you God
I am just like you my father Lord
I am royalty
You put a crown on me
I am goodness
You chose me, Father
I am chosen

Lord expose my flaws
Build me up to correct them
Lord allow me not to get angry
You are the vindicator

I will validate others
And play second fiddle
I will help others whenever I see an opening
Allow me to encourage as often as I can

Excessive words of judgment and criticism
Are so painful Lord
Please allow me to be wise
With my own words
And not give power to other people's words

I thank you Lord for all of your blessings
Large and small
I thank you for everything you provide

Your loving kindness never ceases to amaze me
You are my refuge
I trust you and I am safe
Humble me Father
Humble me at all times.

Let me be satisfied with my lot
Realizing that all you provide
Is not only sufficient
But more than enough
Let me not look at anyone else's life
And feel anything but joy and happiness
For their accomplishments

God, you take care of all of my needs
So if I need it
I have it
If I don't need it
I don't have it
I love you Father
Cover and protect my mind, heart, and tongue
Lord, help me to consciously choose joy
Peace
Happiness
Love
Forgiveness
and Faith

Amen

SHERYL WALKER

The Light

Acceptance
Answered prayer
Awakening
Balance
Belief
Birth
Blessings
Breakthrough
Calling
Celebrations
Change
Chosen
Coincidence
Confidence
Dreams
Epiphany
Eternity
Faith
Family
Freedom
Friends
Gain
Gentleness
Gifts
Giving
Glory
God
God's love
God's presence
Good people that mean you well
Goodness

Graduation
Gratitude
Growth
Happiness
Healing
Health
Hearing from God
His promises
Honesty
Hope
Humility
Inclusion
Justice
Joy
Laughter
Leadership
LOVE
Loving thy neighbor
Marriage
Mercy
Miracles
Obedience
Opportunity
Optimism
Parenting
Patience
Peace
Positivity
Praise
Prayer
Presence

SHERYL WALKER

Promotion

Prosperity

Provision

Purpose

Reconciliation

Rejoice

Retirement

Righteousness

Safety

Salvation

Shifts

Strength

Surrender

Survival

Trust

Understanding

Unity

#1

Never Forgotten

Tortoise legs
Muddled in molasses
Climbing to the top of the hill
Anguished
Careful, cautious, but calculated
When I count the peaks,
The valleys aren't as pronounced
He saves the best for last
From glory to glory
He will never bless you and then leave you

#2

Be the light

Tiny flame
Grandiose illuminator
From the deep dark embers
In the blue-black sky

Let the darkness of man
Cascade into the deafening silhouette
Waking only to the extraneous sounds of cicadas
Feasting on watery tree nectar
Greedy and hard to find

Shine your light
You are the light
Let people see God through you
Your Christ like spirit
Let people know God because of you
Never allow people
In dark places
To take that from you

#3

The elements

TRUST
Hot sticky day
Rain washed skin
Cool and timely
Thank you

FAITH
Clear and composed
The confidence in the darkness
Moon illuminated sergeant at arms of the stars
Thank you

HOPE
Staccato tempo
Cue the drums
Candied rain drops
A little defiant
When will it end?
Thank you

SHERYL WALKER

PURPOSE
What is for me
Is only for me
No one can take that away
No one can alter
God's divine plan for my life
Thank you

#4

Fully whole

Love, sweet love
How I bask in your tender embrace?
Fully whole
Not a want in sight
Oozing with satisfaction
Completion
Connection
Acceptance
Assurance
Glee

#5

The unifier

Baby's dumpling cheeks
All pink gums
No teeth in sight
Tender smile as pronounced as the moon

Ha ha ha
Heeeeeeeeee
Hee hee ahh
Giggle with a head tilt and tears

Furry brown puppy
Frolicking in the window at the pet store
Chasing and barking at the turquoise yarn ball
Pure joy unleashed

Ha ha ha
Heeeeeeeeee
Hee hee ahh
Giggle with a head tilt and tears

Family gathered around the den
With the tattered stained beige rug
Tear ducts filled with liquid
Evoking first the memory, then the sound

Ha
Heeeeeeeeee
Hee hee ahh
Giggle with a head tilt and tears

The depths of a hearty chuckle
Reverberates the hollow core
Moistens eyes
Forming arches like half bitten slices of watermelon

Nothing beats laughter
The joy residue it leaves behind
Like a juicy sweet apple
Picked right from the tree

Speckled banana, too ripe to consume
The archive of memories
With the old friend
Makes the joke that much sweeter
The agreement of humor forms our alliance
That-was-funny

A feeling of belonging
Access never denied
Worries vanish away
If only for four seconds

SHERYL WALKER

#6

Protected

In a cocoon
Safe
Tortoise shell
Armored shield
Things are happening around and to me
But I am protected by a swarm of angels

The weapons and hidden traps,
They have formed
The arrows by day,
They are flying

Lions and wolves,
They are snapping at the heels of the feet
And I step over them

My confidence in you is strong
They will not prosper
No harm will touch me

Unshakable hope that this too shall pass
I am the head and not the tail
I am the beginning and
Not the end

Yesterday is not today and
Today is not yesterday
There is hope in
A brighter day

SHERYL WALKER

#7

Yearning

A season of closed doors
Caught in the cobweb of circumstance
Not even a crumb of opportunity in sight
The harmonica plays a tune of sorrow

Self-pity I don't need you
If God shuts a door
I will not continue to bang on it
Like a dying wasp
Throwing itself into the window's screen
Of an open window
Closed yet open
Possibility of returning to the past
Taunts me

Trusting
That what is behind me
Is no longer meant for me
Brighter days are coming

#8

Puff ball wishes

Lips pursed
Already rejoicing
Exhaling
Parachute seed pods
Escaping
Landing
Hoping
That God will feel
Every blow
Every white fuzz
A different yearning
Dandelion wish granted
Only by God's grace and glory

#9

Bamboo

Bamboo tree
Tall, slender, and enchanting by design
Coiled around the air's temperate frost
A hedge of protection for the mosquito's nest
Majestic even without the sunshine
And even without the rainbow

Magnificent bamboo
After 5 years you begin to grow
Begin. To. Grow.
And in 6 weeks, over 80 feet tall

A miracle
Supernatural miracle
Birthed from a virgin
Parter of the red sea
The loaves of bread multiplied

Time with Christ
Changes you
He's the only one that can mold you
Grow you
Into the admirable opulence
Like the beloved bamboo
Tall, slender, and enchanting by design

SHERYL WALKER

#10

The fountain

Water cycling
In
Up
Through
Back down
Spouting
In and around
Open spaces
I never knew existed
Flowing
Peace filled
Beauty
In the flow
Synchronicity
Of
Time
Space
Reality

#11

Grand life

Grand life, Grand life
You are not in things
But in faith, eternity, and
The simplicity of children
The love of a mother
Believers believing
Pain and sorrow gone
A supernatural provision
The mind cannot conceive

Grand life, Grand life
You are beyond the resources
Beyond the means
An infinite unending
Absolute
Life everlasting
Complete
Composed
Constant

SHERYL WALKER

#12

Eternity

Bustling waterfall
Springing forth
Dancing in the sun's shadow

The fragrant familiarity of family
Buzzing atop daffodils
Fuzzy cloak suffocating goosebumps
In the chill of the night

Waiting for your return
Perfection
Marvel at the
Uninterrupted glorious life
With God forever

#13

Spice of life

Thyme, basil, garlic powder
Fusing together
From bland to aromatic masterpiece
The spice of life

Rainbow adorned sky
We embrace
Squeezing so tightly
Breath limited
Smiles abound
The celebration of your existence
To love and be loved
That is what life is about

Here
Every need met
Job, a daily hell
Family unfamiliar, but
Sun still shining
Still breathing
Still smiling
No lack in sight

Gratitude for each waking day
Contributing
Asking
Still curious
Self-reflecting
Growing
Forgiving
Allowing them to feel forgiven

Reconciliation
A child's laughter
A child's porous mind
Open to life
And possibility
The spice of life
To love and be loved
That is what life is about

#14

Morning

The sun is playing peek-a-boo
"I think the sun wants to play today"
My son says

I see you glorious morning
Another chance to glorify you God
Cherry blossoms blooming

Gratitude for the fragility of life
The blessing to be here
Look around
The splendor
The wind so tender
The clouds so gentle
The shade of the tree so forgiving

How can I not trust you?
How can I not have the utmost faith in you?
Alive and amazed

The magic of a child seeing possibility
In a kite flying high
Or their hugs like a swarm of ants discovering
A half-eaten ice cream cone
On a warm summers' day
Moments of bliss

There is surety
Love is here

Positive
Progressive
Additive
Building
Perfection
Your perfect design
Even in the midst of chaos
You protect me
You love me

Gratitude for the blessings
Gratitude for the lessons
Perfect timing
Place and space
Intended just for me
Oh life
So beautiful

15

The possibilities

Red apple
Yellow apple
Green apple
Pink
Joy in the possibilities

Tulip flower
Daisy flower
Lilac flower
Rose

Start each day
Joyous in the possibilities

Numb spirit
Somber spirit
Hopeless spirit
Sad
Remembering trouble doesn't last always

Surrender to God
Peace through God
Faith in God
Hope
Tomorrow brings a brand-new day of possibilities

#16

Progress

A boulder fixed and unforgiving
Too hard to move

Stuck in the past,
We forget the progress
And all we had to prove

Staring at the thread and needle
Limp and green
Jagged and loose

My Dear,
You are still standing
Be present
Grateful
Joyous
Remain in your groove

#17

Joy in the ordinary

Parched green grass
Yellowing at the top
Banjo playing in the bluegrass band
Bumblebee foraging for nectar and pollen
Hoarding the excess in honeycombs
Red robin
Fresh beginning
Renewal and hope

Find gratitude in the big and small things
Be happy with God
Joy in the everyday
Ordinary things
The grass
The banjo
The red robin
Even the bumble bee

#18

<u>Overcomer</u>

Sunflower
Alone in the field
Smile at the surety
You will win at this life
If He overcame it, so will you
Positive happiness
Is holiness
Connected to God
Boldly, unabashedly
Filled with joy

#19

Proceed

Status quo, no
Even with hazards blinking
Push the chariot forward
Try something new
Discover acorns, leaves, and twigs
In the forest
Even with arrows piercing
Keep seizing each opportunity
Leading with humility
Pressing on

SHERYL WALKER

#20

Where are you God?

Hello summer's sun
Muggy and stale
Fiddle inked story tellers
DVDs, VHS tapes, and cassette players
Open toe shoes
Hair undone

I approach this new day with expectancy and excitement
Moving towards purpose and love

How will God show His face?
Leaves solid green
In the crimson blushing sky

How will He make His presence known?
In the carefree
Embers
Tornadoes
Fireflies
And cranes?

#21

Bonsai

There is beauty in the bonsai
Peace, harmony, and balance in the bonsai
Tenacious strength in the bonsai
Withstands against the elements
People gather round to admire the bonsai
A symbol of simplicity
Of order
An experience of shared admiration
Love for the bonsai
Care for each other
People, experience, love
The investments that multiply

#22

The water

The smell of salty sea water
Tickles the senses
The sound of the waves crashing
Ebbing and flowing
As the water approaches the sand
Sun kissed water
Breeze misty and calculated
Wind dehydrating the skin
Sun rays recharge a sense of peace
Reassurance
A deep knowing
Who controls it all

#23

God's promises

I am crowned with royalty
A living legacy
The heir of His throne
I believe in
His promises
None of us are exempt
If we believe

I will build my faith
On His promises
God's word is sure
What He says will happen
Will happen

His promises are irrevocable
No mid-course corrections
His will reigns supreme

SHERYL WALKER

#24

Joy

Joy, joy
Unspeakable joy
Always dwells within
Despite what is happening
On the outside
An undercurrent of
Pure happiness

#25

Canopy

The sunshine of His love
Is like a canopy
A very special covering

SHERYL WALKER

God

Lord,
Seldom words describe
Your love
Miraculous intentional
Savior
Detailed
Master creator
The prescribed purpose you have set out for our lives
Healer
Comforter
Protector
Burden bearer
Energizer
Hope giver
Vindicator
Battle fighter
Meeter of all needs
Source of strength in times of weariness
The everything, the everywhere
The help in times of trouble
Prince of peace, Lord of Lords
The forgiver of sins
The orchestrator of all good things
God there is no description to adequately capture your
magnitude
Your commitment to your promises
The love you have for us

Grace and mercy giver
Blessings supplier
The joy
The gratitude
Moments of splendor
The gifts
The anointing
The peace
The trust
God, why?
Why do you love us so deeply? And so intensely?
We are so undeserving
Unconditional
L-O-V-E
Steady, firm, and rooted
Thank you, God,
We praise your name
Thank you, God
We glorify you. We honor you.
Thank you, God,
You alone are worthy to be praised

SHERYL WALKER